# THE LIFE-CHANGING JOURNAL

FREEDOM
BOOKWORKS

# *the* LIFE-CHANGING JOURNAL

a 90 day
adventure
to **more love**
happiness
**health** &
wealth

*Skye Baloo*

Edited and Presented by RENA TUCKER

FREEDOM BOOKWORKS
LAS VEGAS, NEVADA, USA

Copyright © 2014 Skye Baloo

Editor: Rena Tucker

Published in the United States of America

This book is not a substitute for medical advice. The author does not advise on, or prescribe, the use of any idea or technique as a substitute for a physician's advice for any medical condition, whether it be physical, emotional, or medical. The sole aim of the author is to offer ideas and general information to help you on your journey toward emotional and spiritual well-being. Neither the author nor the publisher assume any responsibility for your actions as a result of the use of the information contained within this book.

ISBN 13: 978-0-692-26700-4

FREEDOM
BOOKWORKS

www.FreedomBookworks.com

Direct all communications to:

RENAANDSKYE LLC
4952 S. Rainbow Blvd., Suite 280
Las Vegas, NV 89118

Ordering information: Quantity sales. Special discounts are available on quantity purchases by corporations, associations, educational institutions, and others. For details, contact Rena and Skye LLC at the address above.

Cover and Interior Design: Books AND Buck$ - www.BooksAndBucks.com

First Edition, July 2014

THIS IS FOR EVERYONE ON THE JOURNEY

# INTRODUCTION

"To be always intending to make a new and better life, but never to find the time to set about it, is as to put off eating and drinking and sleeping from one day to the next until you're dead."
—OG MANDINO

The great news is that you're no longer merely *intending* to make a better life. You've found an extraordinary tool, *The LIFE-CHANGING JOURNAL*. You're about to experience the simple, yet profound power of asking and answering questions. However, these are no accidental random questions! They've been carefully distilled from years of study as to what truly creates lasting change. You have in your hands the key to **GREATNESS**.

## DON'T WORRY IF YOU MISS A DAY OR TWO...OR THREE...JUST KEEP GOING!

| **TIP:** | If you can set up a buddy system and take 5 minutes a day to share your answers with a friend, they'll have an even greater (and quicker!) impact on your life. |
| --- | --- |

By spending just a few minutes on these questions each day, you'll find your life will undergo an incredible transformation—simply, gently, and *profoundly.*

Can this really work for you? In a word: **YES!!!**

**BUT**...only if you actually **DO IT**.

## "The few who *do* are the envy of the many who only watch."
## —Jim Rohn

"OUR DEEPEST FEAR IS NOT THAT WE ARE INADEQUATE. OUR DEEPEST FEAR IS THAT WE ARE POWERFUL BEYOND MEASURE. IT IS OUR LIGHT, NOT OUR DARKNESS THAT MOST FRIGHTENS US. WE ASK OURSELVES, WHO AM I TO BE BRILLIANT, GORGEOUS, FABULOUS? ACTUALLY, WHO ARE YOU NOT TO BE? YOU ARE A CHILD OF GOD. YOUR PLAYING SMALL DOES NOT SERVE THE WORLD. THERE IS NOTHING ENLIGHTENED ABOUT SHRINKING SO THAT OTHER PEOPLE WON'T FEEL INSECURE AROUND YOU. WE ARE ALL MEANT TO SHINE, AS CHILDREN DO. WE WERE BORN TO MAKE MANIFEST THE GLORY OF GOD THAT IS WITHIN US. IT'S NOT JUST IN SOME OF US; IT'S IN EVERYONE. AND AS WE LET OUR OWN LIGHT SHINE, WE UNCONSCIOUSLY GIVE OTHER PEOPLE PERMISSION TO DO THE SAME. AS WE ARE LIBERATED FROM OUR OWN FEAR, OUR PRESENCE AUTOMATICALLY LIBERATES OTHERS."

—FROM *A RETURN TO LOVE*, BY MARIANNE WILLIAMSON

# HOW TO USE YOUR JOURNAL

The *LIFE-CHANGING JOURNAL* centers around a set of questions you'll answer every day.

Make time for your journaling, both in the morning, and in the evening. It could be as little as 5 minutes or as much as an hour, but it's the *doing* of it that will turn your life around.

## MORNING : THE LIFE CHANGING QUESTIONS

Devise a set of 5 questions to ask yourself every day, ideally sharing this exercise with a colleague or someone else on the journey. You'll find that by simply **ASKING** these questions each day you'll begin to change your life in small and large ways.

Motivational superstars **TONY ROBBINS** and **BRENDON BURCHARD** both ask themselves:

— **What am I excited about today?**

— **What am I grateful for?**

— **What am I committed to?**

Those are good staples, so I ask myself those questions, too. **The additional questions I ask are:**

— **What brings me the most joy right now in my life?**

— **What area of growth is bringing me the most relief right now in my life?**

OF COURSE, FEEL FREE TO ASK YOURSELF WHATEVER WORKS BEST FOR <u>YOU</u>.

Once you've answered each question, ask **what is it about THAT** (your answer), that gets you to be **excited, grateful, committed, etc.** Finally, ask yourself **how it makes you FEEL.**

FOR EXAMPLE:

What am I excited about today? *Going to the lake with friends.*

What is it about *that* that gets me so excited? *Floating on an inflatable raft and tossing a beach ball.*

How does that make me feel? *Like a kid again!*

The reason it's **SO IMPORTANT** to ask yourself how it makes you feel is that it's *never the thing itself* that's wonderful. All any of us are looking for is a better way to feel.

There's a really interesting fact of life: Being rich or successful **doesn't make us happy**. Being fit, gorgeous, etc. doesn't, either. People can tell you they love you—or they hate you—and **even** *that* isn't the essence of a life change.

What really changes your life is when you **do something difficult** that you know you need to do, and push yourself through it. Again, it isn't **what** you do that changes your life. It's the **feeling** you get when you do it that changes everything. You feel pride, and a sense of accomplishment...and something even **greater** than that: The feeling of **"BEING"** at last—living the potential of all you were created to be—and the feeling of **aliveness** as a result. That feeling will get you through *anything*.

So, each day, pick **two challenging tasks** to tackle. If a task is something you can *finish*—like making a phone call—do it! If it's part of working toward a goal, **decide how much** you want to achieve today and GO FOR IT!

# IN THE EVENING: WRAP UP TODAY'S LIFE CHANGE

It's all **too EASY** to list our faults or failings. Most of us can write volumes on this in a *nanosecond*.

What's **far** more challenging is listing our GOOD POINTS.

Here's a GREAT exercise, which, again, will change your life:

Every evening, write down FIVE different COMPLIMENTS about yourself.

The COMPLIMENTS might be about the way you handled a situation, helped someone, or accomplished a task.

By doing this, you learn to LIVE WITH LOVE FOR YOURSELF, and this is the basis for everything.

# FINALLY: THE "WILDEST DREAMS" QUESTIONS

These questions will help you get to know yourself better and prepare you for the quality of life you're working toward, which is soon to happen: The one in which you live the life of your **wildest dreams!**

THE QUESTIONS ARE:

—**When did I feel alive today? Describe that feeling!**
—**What did I love today? And who/what loved me?**
—**When did time fly today?**
—**What are my dreams?**

# LET'S GET STARTED...

SO YOU'LL BE READY TO GO ON MONDAY, WRITE DOWN
YOUR FIVE MORNING QUESTIONS BELOW.

## FIVE QUESTIONS I'LL ASK MYSELF EVERY MORNING:

1. ~~What is one thing, of o out of the Many things,~~
   Whats one thing I am grateful for (right now?)

2. Whats an area of growth I'm really excited about tackling today?

3. What is one thing I can do today to bring another joy?

4. One way to describe myself today (positives only)

5. One thing I can do today that will help me move closer to
   a goal (think simple)

## IN CASE YOU WROTE IN PEN AND MESSED UP, HERE'S YOUR DO-OVER...

1.

2.

3.

4.

5.

Now you're ready!

Let the life changing begin...

# DAY 1

## ANSWERS TO MY MORNING QUESTIONS:

Answer 1: I am grateful for spending time w/ Brayden + Briley this weekend?

What is it about *that?*
I get to see them learn + grow.

How does it make me feel?
It makes me happy to see them become more complex.

Answer 2: Today I'd really like to tackle relaxation.

What is it about *that?*
Lately I've been stressed + not much time to myself

How does it make me feel?
It makes me even more grateful to be with others.

Answer 3: Be grateful to them.

What is it about *that?*
I like bringing others joy or comfort.

How does it make me feel?
It makes to feel like I am a comforty person.

Answer 4: Chill

What is it about *that?*
Today I chilled really hard

How does it make me feel?
Regenerated, Ready.

Answer 5: Relax + drink water.

What is it about *that?*
Doing this was helpful to me right now.

How does it make me feel?
Regenerated, Ready

## TWO CHALLENGING TASKS FOR TODAY:

1. Go to sleep early

2. Read.

# DATE _____

EVENING WRAP-UP:

FIVE COMPLIMENTS:

1.

2.

3.

4.

5.

## THE "WILDEST DREAMS" QUESTIONS:

1. When did I feel alive today?  (Describe the feeling!)

2. What did I love today? And who/what loved me?

3. When did time fly today?

4. What are my dreams?

## ANSWERS TO MY MORNING QUESTIONS:

**Answer 1:**

What is it about *that?*

How does it make me feel?

**Answer 2:**

What is it about *that?*

How does it make me feel?

**Answer 3:**

What is it about *that?*

How does it make me feel?

**Answer 4:**

What is it about *that?*

How does it make me feel?

**Answer 5:**

What is it about *that?*

How does it make me feel?

## TWO CHALLENGING TASKS FOR TODAY:

1.

2.

# DATE _____

EVENING WRAP-UP:

FIVE COMPLIMENTS:

1.

2.

3.

4.

5.

## THE "WILDEST DREAMS" QUESTIONS:

1. When did I feel alive today?  (Describe the feeling!)

2. What did I love today? And who/what loved me?

3. When did time fly today?

4. What are my dreams?

## ANSWERS TO MY MORNING QUESTIONS:

**Answer 1:**

What is it about *that?*

How does it make me feel?

**Answer 2:**

What is it about *that?*

How does it make me feel?

**Answer 3:**

What is it about *that?*

How does it make me feel?

**Answer 4:**

What is it about *that?*

How does it make me feel?

**Answer 5:**

What is it about *that?*

How does it make me feel?

## TWO CHALLENGING TASKS FOR TODAY:

1.

2.

# DATE _____

EVENING WRAP-UP:

FIVE COMPLIMENTS:

1.

2.

3.

4.

5.

## THE "WILDEST DREAMS" QUESTIONS:

1. When did I feel alive today?  (Describe the feeling!)


2. What did I love today? And who/what loved me?


3. When did time fly today?


4. What are my dreams?

## ANSWERS TO MY MORNING QUESTIONS:

**Answer 1:**

What is it about *that?*

How does it make me feel?

**Answer 2:**

What is it about *that?*

How does it make me feel?

**Answer 3:**

What is it about *that?*

How does it make me feel?

**Answer 4:**

What is it about *that?*

How does it make me feel?

**Answer 5:**

What is it about *that?*

How does it make me feel?

## TWO CHALLENGING TASKS FOR TODAY:

1.

2.

# DATE _____

EVENING WRAP-UP:

FIVE COMPLIMENTS:

1.

2.

3.

4.

5.

## THE "WILDEST DREAMS" QUESTIONS:

1. When did I feel alive today?  (Describe the feeling!)



2. What did I love today? And who/what loved me?



3. When did time fly today?



4. What are my dreams?

## ANSWERS TO MY MORNING QUESTIONS:

**Answer 1:**

What is it about *that?*

How does it make me feel?

**Answer 2:**

What is it about *that?*

How does it make me feel?

**Answer 3:**

What is it about *that?*

How does it make me feel?

**Answer 4:**

What is it about *that?*

How does it make me feel?

**Answer 5:**

What is it about *that?*

How does it make me feel?

## TWO CHALLENGING TASKS FOR TODAY:

1.

2.

# DATE _____

EVENING WRAP-UP:

FIVE COMPLIMENTS:

1.

2.

3.

4.

5.

## THE "WILDEST DREAMS" QUESTIONS:

1. When did I feel alive today? (Describe the feeling!)

2. What did I love today? And who/what loved me?

3. When did time fly today?

4. What are my dreams?

## ANSWERS TO MY MORNING QUESTIONS:

**Answer 1:**

What is it about *that?*

How does it make me feel?

**Answer 2:**

What is it about *that?*

How does it make me feel?

**Answer 3:**

What is it about *that?*

How does it make me feel?

**Answer 4:**

What is it about *that?*

How does it make me feel?

**Answer 5:**

What is it about *that?*

How does it make me feel?

## TWO CHALLENGING TASKS FOR TODAY:

1.

2.

# DATE _____

EVENING WRAP-UP:

FIVE COMPLIMENTS:

1.

2.

3.

4.

5.

## THE "WILDEST DREAMS" QUESTIONS:

1. When did I feel alive today?  (Describe the feeling!)

2. What did I love today? And who/what loved me?

3. When did time fly today?

4. What are my dreams?

## ANSWERS TO MY MORNING QUESTIONS:

**Answer 1:**

What is it about *that?*

How does it make me feel?

**Answer 2:**

What is it about *that?*

How does it make me feel?

**Answer 3:**

What is it about *that?*

How does it make me feel?

**Answer 4:**

What is it about *that?*

How does it make me feel?

**Answer 5:**

What is it about *that?*

How does it make me feel?

## TWO CHALLENGING TASKS FOR TODAY:

1.

2.

# DATE _____

EVENING WRAP-UP:

FIVE COMPLIMENTS:

1.

2.

3.

4.

5.

## THE "WILDEST DREAMS" QUESTIONS:

1. When did I feel alive today?  (Describe the feeling!)

2. What did I love today? And who/what loved me?

3. When did time fly today?

4. What are my dreams?

## ANSWERS TO MY MORNING QUESTIONS:

**Answer 1:**

What is it about *that?*

How does it make me feel?

**Answer 2:**

What is it about *that?*

How does it make me feel?

**Answer 3:**

What is it about *that?*

How does it make me feel?

**Answer 4:**

What is it about *that?*

How does it make me feel?

**Answer 5:**

What is it about *that?*

How does it make me feel?

## TWO CHALLENGING TASKS FOR TODAY:

1.

2.

# DATE _____

EVENING WRAP-UP:

FIVE COMPLIMENTS:

1.

2.

3.

4.

5.

## THE "WILDEST DREAMS" QUESTIONS:

1. When did I feel alive today?  (Describe the feeling!)

2. What did I love today? And who/what loved me?

3. When did time fly today?

4. What are my dreams?

## ANSWERS TO MY MORNING QUESTIONS:

**Answer 1:**

What is it about *that?*

How does it make me feel?

**Answer 2:**

What is it about *that?*

How does it make me feel?

**Answer 3:**

What is it about *that?*

How does it make me feel?

**Answer 4:**

What is it about *that?*

How does it make me feel?

**Answer 5:**

What is it about *that?*

How does it make me feel?

## TWO CHALLENGING TASKS FOR TODAY:

1.

2.

# DATE _____

EVENING WRAP-UP:

FIVE COMPLIMENTS:

1.

2.

3.

4.

5.

## THE "WILDEST DREAMS" QUESTIONS:

1. When did I feel alive today?  (Describe the feeling!)

2. What did I love today? And who/what loved me?

3. When did time fly today?

4. What are my dreams?

## ANSWERS TO MY MORNING QUESTIONS:

**Answer 1:**

What is it about *that?*

How does it make me feel?

**Answer 2:**

What is it about *that?*

How does it make me feel?

**Answer 3:**

What is it about *that?*

How does it make me feel?

**Answer 4:**

What is it about *that?*

How does it make me feel?

**Answer 5:**

What is it about *that?*

How does it make me feel?

## TWO CHALLENGING TASKS FOR TODAY:

1.

2.

# DATE _____

EVENING WRAP-UP:

FIVE COMPLIMENTS:

1.

2.

3.

4.

5.

## THE "WILDEST DREAMS" QUESTIONS:

1. When did I feel alive today?  (Describe the feeling!)


2. What did I love today? And who/what loved me?


3. When did time fly today?


4. What are my dreams?

## ANSWERS TO MY MORNING QUESTIONS:

**Answer 1:**

What is it about *that?*

How does it make me feel?

**Answer 2:**

What is it about *that?*

How does it make me feel?

**Answer 3:**

What is it about *that?*

How does it make me feel?

**Answer 4:**

What is it about *that?*

How does it make me feel?

**Answer 5:**

What is it about *that?*

How does it make me feel?

## TWO CHALLENGING TASKS FOR TODAY:

1.

2.

# DATE _____

EVENING WRAP-UP:

FIVE COMPLIMENTS:

1.

2.

3.

4.

5.

## THE "WILDEST DREAMS" QUESTIONS:

1. When did I feel alive today?  (Describe the feeling!)

2. What did I love today? And who/what loved me?

3. When did time fly today?

4. What are my dreams?

## ANSWERS TO MY MORNING QUESTIONS:

**Answer 1:**

What is it about *that?*

How does it make me feel?

**Answer 2:**

What is it about *that?*

How does it make me feel?

**Answer 3:**

What is it about *that?*

How does it make me feel?

**Answer 4:**

What is it about *that?*

How does it make me feel?

**Answer 5:**

What is it about *that?*

How does it make me feel?

## TWO CHALLENGING TASKS FOR TODAY:

1.

2.

# DATE _____

EVENING WRAP-UP:

FIVE COMPLIMENTS:

1.

2.

3.

4.

5.

## THE "WILDEST DREAMS" QUESTIONS:

1. When did I feel alive today?  (Describe the feeling!)

2. What did I love today? And who/what loved me?

3. When did time fly today?

4. What are my dreams?

## ANSWERS TO MY MORNING QUESTIONS:

**Answer 1:**

What is it about *that?*

How does it make me feel?

**Answer 2:**

What is it about *that?*

How does it make me feel?

**Answer 3:**

What is it about *that?*

How does it make me feel?

**Answer 4:**

What is it about *that?*

How does it make me feel?

**Answer 5:**

What is it about *that?*

How does it make me feel?

## TWO CHALLENGING TASKS FOR TODAY:

1.

2.

# DATE _____

EVENING WRAP-UP:

FIVE COMPLIMENTS:

1.

2.

3.

4.

5.

## THE "WILDEST DREAMS" QUESTIONS:

1. When did I feel alive today?  (Describe the feeling!)

2. What did I love today? And who/what loved me?

3. When did time fly today?

4. What are my dreams?

## ANSWERS TO MY MORNING QUESTIONS:

**Answer 1:**

What is it about *that?*

How does it make me feel?

**Answer 2:**

What is it about *that?*

How does it make me feel?

**Answer 3:**

What is it about *that?*

How does it make me feel?

**Answer 4:**

What is it about *that?*

How does it make me feel?

**Answer 5:**

What is it about *that?*

How does it make me feel?

## TWO CHALLENGING TASKS FOR TODAY:

1.

2.

# DATE _____

EVENING WRAP-UP:

FIVE COMPLIMENTS:

1.

2.

3.

4.

5.

## THE "WILDEST DREAMS" QUESTIONS:

1. When did I feel alive today?  (Describe the feeling!)

2. What did I love today? And who/what loved me?

3. When did time fly today?

4. What are my dreams?

## ANSWERS TO MY MORNING QUESTIONS:

**Answer 1:**

What is it about *that?*

How does it make me feel?

**Answer 2:**

What is it about *that?*

How does it make me feel?

**Answer 3:**

What is it about *that?*

How does it make me feel?

**Answer 4:**

What is it about *that?*

How does it make me feel?

**Answer 5:**

What is it about *that?*

How does it make me feel?

## TWO CHALLENGING TASKS FOR TODAY:

1.

2.

# DATE _____

EVENING WRAP-UP:

FIVE COMPLIMENTS:

1.

2.

3.

4.

5.

## THE "WILDEST DREAMS" QUESTIONS:

1. When did I feel alive today?  (Describe the feeling!)




2. What did I love today? And who/what loved me?




3. When did time fly today?




4. What are my dreams?

## ANSWERS TO MY MORNING QUESTIONS:

**Answer 1:**

What is it about *that?*

How does it make me feel?

**Answer 2:**

What is it about *that?*

How does it make me feel?

**Answer 3:**

What is it about *that?*

How does it make me feel?

**Answer 4:**

What is it about *that?*

How does it make me feel?

**Answer 5:**

What is it about *that?*

How does it make me feel?

## TWO CHALLENGING TASKS FOR TODAY:

1.

2.

# DATE _____

EVENING WRAP-UP:

FIVE COMPLIMENTS:

1.

2.

3.

4.

5.

## THE "WILDEST DREAMS" QUESTIONS:

1. When did I feel alive today?  (Describe the feeling!)

2. What did I love today? And who/what loved me?

3. When did time fly today?

4. What are my dreams?

## ANSWERS TO MY MORNING QUESTIONS:

**Answer 1:**

What is it about *that?*

How does it make me feel?

**Answer 2:**

What is it about *that?*

How does it make me feel?

**Answer 3:**

What is it about *that?*

How does it make me feel?

**Answer 4:**

What is it about *that?*

How does it make me feel?

**Answer 5:**

What is it about *that?*

How does it make me feel?

## TWO CHALLENGING TASKS FOR TODAY:

1.

2.

# DATE _____

EVENING WRAP-UP:

FIVE COMPLIMENTS:

1.

2.

3.

4.

5.

## THE "WILDEST DREAMS" QUESTIONS:

1. When did I feel alive today?  (Describe the feeling!)


2. What did I love today? And who/what loved me?


3. When did time fly today?


4. What are my dreams?

# DAY 18

## ANSWERS TO MY MORNING QUESTIONS:

**Answer 1:**

What is it about *that?*

How does it make me feel?

**Answer 2:**

What is it about *that?*

How does it make me feel?

**Answer 3:**

What is it about *that?*

How does it make me feel?

**Answer 4:**

What is it about *that?*

How does it make me feel?

**Answer 5:**

What is it about *that?*

How does it make me feel?

## TWO CHALLENGING TASKS FOR TODAY:

1.

2.

# DATE _____

EVENING WRAP-UP:

FIVE COMPLIMENTS:

1.

2.

3.

4.

5.

## THE "WILDEST DREAMS" QUESTIONS:

1. When did I feel alive today?  (Describe the feeling!)



2. What did I love today? And who/what loved me?



3. When did time fly today?



4. What are my dreams?

## ANSWERS TO MY MORNING QUESTIONS:

**Answer 1:**

What is it about *that?*

How does it make me feel?

**Answer 2:**

What is it about *that?*

How does it make me feel?

**Answer 3:**

What is it about *that?*

How does it make me feel?

**Answer 4:**

What is it about *that?*

How does it make me feel?

**Answer 5:**

What is it about *that?*

How does it make me feel?

## TWO CHALLENGING TASKS FOR TODAY:

1.

2.

# DATE _____

EVENING WRAP-UP:

FIVE COMPLIMENTS:

1.

2.

3.

4.

5.

## THE "WILDEST DREAMS" QUESTIONS:

1. When did I feel alive today?  (Describe the feeling!)

2. What did I love today? And who/what loved me?

3. When did time fly today?

4. What are my dreams?

## ANSWERS TO MY MORNING QUESTIONS:

**Answer 1:**

What is it about *that?*

How does it make me feel?

**Answer 2:**

What is it about *that?*

How does it make me feel?

**Answer 3:**

What is it about *that?*

How does it make me feel?

**Answer 4:**

What is it about *that?*

How does it make me feel?

**Answer 5:**

What is it about *that?*

How does it make me feel?

## TWO CHALLENGING TASKS FOR TODAY:

1.

2.

# DATE _____

EVENING WRAP-UP:

FIVE COMPLIMENTS:

1.

2.

3.

4.

5.

## THE "WILDEST DREAMS" QUESTIONS:

1. When did I feel alive today?  (Describe the feeling!)

2. What did I love today? And who/what loved me?

3. When did time fly today?

4. What are my dreams?

## ANSWERS TO MY MORNING QUESTIONS:

**Answer 1:**

What is it about *that?*

How does it make me feel?

**Answer 2:**

What is it about *that?*

How does it make me feel?

**Answer 3:**

What is it about *that?*

How does it make me feel?

**Answer 4:**

What is it about *that?*

How does it make me feel?

**Answer 5:**

What is it about *that?*

How does it make me feel?

## TWO CHALLENGING TASKS FOR TODAY:

1.

2.

# DATE _____

EVENING WRAP-UP:

FIVE COMPLIMENTS:

1.

2.

3.

4.

5.


## THE "WILDEST DREAMS" QUESTIONS:

1. When did I feel alive today?  (Describe the feeling!)




2. What did I love today? And who/what loved me?




3. When did time fly today?




4. What are my dreams?

## ANSWERS TO MY MORNING QUESTIONS:

**Answer 1:**

What is it about *that?*

How does it make me feel?

**Answer 2:**

What is it about *that?*

How does it make me feel?

**Answer 3:**

What is it about *that?*

How does it make me feel?

**Answer 4:**

What is it about *that?*

How does it make me feel?

**Answer 5:**

What is it about *that?*

How does it make me feel?

## TWO CHALLENGING TASKS FOR TODAY:

1.

2.

# DATE _____

EVENING WRAP-UP:

FIVE COMPLIMENTS:

1.

2.

3.

4.

5.

## THE "WILDEST DREAMS" QUESTIONS:

1. When did I feel alive today?  (Describe the feeling!)

2. What did I love today? And who/what loved me?

3. When did time fly today?

4. What are my dreams?

## ANSWERS TO MY MORNING QUESTIONS:

**Answer 1:**

What is it about *that?*

How does it make me feel?

**Answer 2:**

What is it about *that?*

How does it make me feel?

**Answer 3:**

What is it about *that?*

How does it make me feel?

**Answer 4:**

What is it about *that?*

How does it make me feel?

**Answer 5:**

What is it about *that?*

How does it make me feel?

## TWO CHALLENGING TASKS FOR TODAY:

1.

2.

# DATE _____

EVENING WRAP-UP:

FIVE COMPLIMENTS:

1.

2.

3.

4.

5.

## THE "WILDEST DREAMS" QUESTIONS:

1. When did I feel alive today?  (Describe the feeling!)



2. What did I love today? And who/what loved me?



3. When did time fly today?



4. What are my dreams?

## ANSWERS TO MY MORNING QUESTIONS:

**Answer 1:**

What is it about *that?*

How does it make me feel?

**Answer 2:**

What is it about *that?*

How does it make me feel?

**Answer 3:**

What is it about *that?*

How does it make me feel?

**Answer 4:**

What is it about *that?*

How does it make me feel?

**Answer 5:**

What is it about *that?*

How does it make me feel?

## TWO CHALLENGING TASKS FOR TODAY:

1.

2.

# DATE _____

EVENING WRAP-UP:

FIVE COMPLIMENTS:

1.

2.

3.

4.

5.

## THE "WILDEST DREAMS" QUESTIONS:

1. When did I feel alive today?  (Describe the feeling!)



2. What did I love today? And who/what loved me?



3. When did time fly today?



4. What are my dreams?

## ANSWERS TO MY MORNING QUESTIONS:

**Answer 1:**

What is it about *that?*

How does it make me feel?

**Answer 2:**

What is it about *that?*

How does it make me feel?

**Answer 3:**

What is it about *that?*

How does it make me feel?

**Answer 4:**

What is it about *that?*

How does it make me feel?

**Answer 5:**

What is it about *that?*

How does it make me feel?

## TWO CHALLENGING TASKS FOR TODAY:

1.

2.

# DATE _____

EVENING WRAP-UP:

FIVE COMPLIMENTS:

1.

2.

3.

4.

5.

## THE "WILDEST DREAMS" QUESTIONS:

1. When did I feel alive today?  (Describe the feeling!)

2. What did I love today? And who/what loved me?

3. When did time fly today?

4. What are my dreams?

## ANSWERS TO MY MORNING QUESTIONS:

**Answer 1:**

What is it about *that?*

How does it make me feel?

**Answer 2:**

What is it about *that?*

How does it make me feel?

**Answer 3:**

What is it about *that?*

How does it make me feel?

**Answer 4:**

What is it about *that?*

How does it make me feel?

**Answer 5:**

What is it about *that?*

How does it make me feel?

## TWO CHALLENGING TASKS FOR TODAY:

1.

2.

# DATE _____

EVENING WRAP-UP:

FIVE COMPLIMENTS:

1.

2.

3.

4.

5.

## THE "WILDEST DREAMS" QUESTIONS:

1. When did I feel alive today?  (Describe the feeling!)

2. What did I love today? And who/what loved me?

3. When did time fly today?

4. What are my dreams?

## ANSWERS TO MY MORNING QUESTIONS:

**Answer 1:**

What is it about *that?*

How does it make me feel?

**Answer 2:**

What is it about *that?*

How does it make me feel?

**Answer 3:**

What is it about *that?*

How does it make me feel?

**Answer 4:**

What is it about *that?*

How does it make me feel?

**Answer 5:**

What is it about *that?*

How does it make me feel?

## TWO CHALLENGING TASKS FOR TODAY:

1.

2.

# DATE _____

EVENING WRAP-UP:

FIVE COMPLIMENTS:

1.

2.

3.

4.

5.

## THE "WILDEST DREAMS" QUESTIONS:

1. When did I feel alive today?  (Describe the feeling!)

2. What did I love today? And who/what loved me?

3. When did time fly today?

4. What are my dreams?

## ANSWERS TO MY MORNING QUESTIONS:

**Answer 1:**

What is it about *that?*

How does it make me feel?

**Answer 2:**

What is it about *that?*

How does it make me feel?

**Answer 3:**

What is it about *that?*

How does it make me feel?

**Answer 4:**

What is it about *that?*

How does it make me feel?

**Answer 5:**

What is it about *that?*

How does it make me feel?

## TWO CHALLENGING TASKS FOR TODAY:

1.

2.

# DATE _____

EVENING WRAP-UP:

FIVE COMPLIMENTS:

1.

2.

3.

4.

5.

## THE "WILDEST DREAMS" QUESTIONS:

1. When did I feel alive today? (Describe the feeling!)

2. What did I love today? And who/what loved me?

3. When did time fly today?

4. What are my dreams?

## ANSWERS TO MY MORNING QUESTIONS:

**Answer 1:**

What is it about *that?*

How does it make me feel?

**Answer 2:**

What is it about *that?*

How does it make me feel?

**Answer 3:**

What is it about *that?*

How does it make me feel?

**Answer 4:**

What is it about *that?*

How does it make me feel?

**Answer 5:**

What is it about *that?*

How does it make me feel?

## TWO CHALLENGING TASKS FOR TODAY:

1.

2.

# DATE _____

EVENING WRAP-UP:

FIVE COMPLIMENTS:

1.

2.

3.

4.

5.

## THE "WILDEST DREAMS" QUESTIONS:

1. When did I feel alive today?  (Describe the feeling!)

2. What did I love today? And who/what loved me?

3. When did time fly today?

4. What are my dreams?

## ANSWERS TO MY MORNING QUESTIONS:

**Answer 1:**

What is it about *that?*

How does it make me feel?

**Answer 2:**

What is it about *that?*

How does it make me feel?

**Answer 3:**

What is it about *that?*

How does it make me feel?

**Answer 4:**

What is it about *that?*

How does it make me feel?

**Answer 5:**

What is it about *that?*

How does it make me feel?

## TWO CHALLENGING TASKS FOR TODAY:

1.

2.

# DATE _____

EVENING WRAP-UP:

FIVE COMPLIMENTS:

1.

2.

3.

4.

5.

## THE "WILDEST DREAMS" QUESTIONS:

1. When did I feel alive today?  (Describe the feeling!)

2. What did I love today? And who/what loved me?

3. When did time fly today?

4. What are my dreams?

## ANSWERS TO MY MORNING QUESTIONS:

**Answer 1:**

What is it about *that?*

How does it make me feel?

**Answer 2:**

What is it about *that?*

How does it make me feel?

**Answer 3:**

What is it about *that?*

How does it make me feel?

**Answer 4:**

What is it about *that?*

How does it make me feel?

**Answer 5:**

What is it about *that?*

How does it make me feel?

## TWO CHALLENGING TASKS FOR TODAY:

1.

2.

# DATE _____

EVENING WRAP-UP:

FIVE COMPLIMENTS:

1.

2.

3.

4.

5.

## THE "WILDEST DREAMS" QUESTIONS:

1. When did I feel alive today? (Describe the feeling!)




2. What did I love today? And who/what loved me?




3. When did time fly today?




4. What are my dreams?

## ANSWERS TO MY MORNING QUESTIONS:

**Answer 1:**

What is it about *that?*

How does it make me feel?

**Answer 2:**

What is it about *that?*

How does it make me feel?

**Answer 3:**

What is it about *that?*

How does it make me feel?

**Answer 4:**

What is it about *that?*

How does it make me feel?

**Answer 5:**

What is it about *that?*

How does it make me feel?

## TWO CHALLENGING TASKS FOR TODAY:

1.

2.

# DATE _____

EVENING WRAP-UP:

FIVE COMPLIMENTS:

1.

2.

3.

4.

5.

## THE "WILDEST DREAMS" QUESTIONS:

1. When did I feel alive today?  (Describe the feeling!)



2. What did I love today? And who/what loved me?



3. When did time fly today?



4. What are my dreams?

## ANSWERS TO MY MORNING QUESTIONS:

**Answer 1:**

What is it about *that?*

How does it make me feel?

**Answer 2:**

What is it about *that?*

How does it make me feel?

**Answer 3:**

What is it about *that?*

How does it make me feel?

**Answer 4:**

What is it about *that?*

How does it make me feel?

**Answer 5:**

What is it about *that?*

How does it make me feel?

## TWO CHALLENGING TASKS FOR TODAY:

1.

2.

# DATE _____

EVENING WRAP-UP:

FIVE COMPLIMENTS:

1.

2.

3.

4.

5.

## THE "WILDEST DREAMS" QUESTIONS:

1. When did I feel alive today?  (Describe the feeling!)

2. What did I love today? And who/what loved me?

3. When did time fly today?

4. What are my dreams?

## ANSWERS TO MY MORNING QUESTIONS:

**Answer 1:**

What is it about *that?*

How does it make me feel?

**Answer 2:**

What is it about *that?*

How does it make me feel?

**Answer 3:**

What is it about *that?*

How does it make me feel?

**Answer 4:**

What is it about *that?*

How does it make me feel?

**Answer 5:**

What is it about *that?*

How does it make me feel?

## TWO CHALLENGING TASKS FOR TODAY:

1.

2.

# DATE _____

EVENING WRAP-UP:

FIVE COMPLIMENTS:

1.

2.

3.

4.

5.

## THE "WILDEST DREAMS" QUESTIONS:

1. When did I feel alive today?  (Describe the feeling!)


2. What did I love today? And who/what loved me?


3. When did time fly today?


4. What are my dreams?

## ANSWERS TO MY MORNING QUESTIONS:

**Answer 1:**

What is it about *that?*

How does it make me feel?

**Answer 2:**

What is it about *that?*

How does it make me feel?

**Answer 3:**

What is it about *that?*

How does it make me feel?

**Answer 4:**

What is it about *that?*

How does it make me feel?

**Answer 5:**

What is it about *that?*

How does it make me feel?

## TWO CHALLENGING TASKS FOR TODAY:

1.

2.

# DATE _____

EVENING WRAP-UP:

FIVE COMPLIMENTS:

1.

2.

3.

4.

5.

## THE "WILDEST DREAMS" QUESTIONS:

1. When did I feel alive today?  (Describe the feeling!)

2. What did I love today? And who/what loved me?

3. When did time fly today?

4. What are my dreams?

## ANSWERS TO MY MORNING QUESTIONS:

**Answer 1:**

What is it about *that?*

How does it make me feel?

**Answer 2:**

What is it about *that?*

How does it make me feel?

**Answer 3:**

What is it about *that?*

How does it make me feel?

**Answer 4:**

What is it about *that?*

How does it make me feel?

**Answer 5:**

What is it about *that?*

How does it make me feel?

## TWO CHALLENGING TASKS FOR TODAY:

1.

2.

# DATE _____

EVENING WRAP-UP:

FIVE COMPLIMENTS:

1.

2.

3.

4.

5.

## THE "WILDEST DREAMS" QUESTIONS:

1. When did I feel alive today?  (Describe the feeling!)

2. What did I love today? And who/what loved me?

3. When did time fly today?

4. What are my dreams?

## ANSWERS TO MY MORNING QUESTIONS:

**Answer 1:**

What is it about *that?*

How does it make me feel?

**Answer 2:**

What is it about *that?*

How does it make me feel?

**Answer 3:**

What is it about *that?*

How does it make me feel?

**Answer 4:**

What is it about *that?*

How does it make me feel?

**Answer 5:**

What is it about *that?*

How does it make me feel?

## TWO CHALLENGING TASKS FOR TODAY:

1.

2.

# DATE _____

EVENING WRAP-UP:

FIVE COMPLIMENTS:

1.

2.

3.

4.

5.

## THE "WILDEST DREAMS" QUESTIONS:

1. When did I feel alive today?  (Describe the feeling!)

2. What did I love today? And who/what loved me?

3. When did time fly today?

4. What are my dreams?

## ANSWERS TO MY MORNING QUESTIONS:

**Answer 1:**

What is it about *that?*

How does it make me feel?

**Answer 2:**

What is it about *that?*

How does it make me feel?

**Answer 3:**

What is it about *that?*

How does it make me feel?

**Answer 4:**

What is it about *that?*

How does it make me feel?

**Answer 5:**

What is it about *that?*

How does it make me feel?

## TWO CHALLENGING TASKS FOR TODAY:

1.

2.

# DATE _____

EVENING WRAP-UP:

FIVE COMPLIMENTS:

1.

2.

3.

4.

5.

## THE "WILDEST DREAMS" QUESTIONS:

1. When did I feel alive today?  (Describe the feeling!)

2. What did I love today? And who/what loved me?

3. When did time fly today?

4. What are my dreams?

## ANSWERS TO MY MORNING QUESTIONS:

**Answer 1:**

What is it about *that?*

How does it make me feel?

**Answer 2:**

What is it about *that?*

How does it make me feel?

**Answer 3:**

What is it about *that?*

How does it make me feel?

**Answer 4:**

What is it about *that?*

How does it make me feel?

**Answer 5:**

What is it about *that?*

How does it make me feel?

## TWO CHALLENGING TASKS FOR TODAY:

1.

2.

# DATE _____

EVENING WRAP-UP:

FIVE COMPLIMENTS:

1.

2.

3.

4.

5.

## THE "WILDEST DREAMS" QUESTIONS:

1. When did I feel alive today?  (Describe the feeling!)

2. What did I love today? And who/what loved me?

3. When did time fly today?

4. What are my dreams?

## ANSWERS TO MY MORNING QUESTIONS:

**Answer 1:**

What is it about *that?*

How does it make me feel?

**Answer 2:**

What is it about *that?*

How does it make me feel?

**Answer 3:**

What is it about *that?*

How does it make me feel?

**Answer 4:**

What is it about *that?*

How does it make me feel?

**Answer 5:**

What is it about *that?*

How does it make me feel?

## TWO CHALLENGING TASKS FOR TODAY:

1.

2.

# DATE _____

EVENING WRAP-UP:

FIVE COMPLIMENTS:

1.

2.

3.

4.

5.

## THE "WILDEST DREAMS" QUESTIONS:

1. When did I feel alive today?  (Describe the feeling!)


2. What did I love today? And who/what loved me?


3. When did time fly today?


4. What are my dreams?

## ANSWERS TO MY MORNING QUESTIONS:

**Answer 1:**

What is it about *that?*

How does it make me feel?

**Answer 2:**

What is it about *that?*

How does it make me feel?

**Answer 3:**

What is it about *that?*

How does it make me feel?

**Answer 4:**

What is it about *that?*

How does it make me feel?

**Answer 5:**

What is it about *that?*

How does it make me feel?


## TWO CHALLENGING TASKS FOR TODAY:

1.

2.

# DATE _____

EVENING WRAP-UP:

FIVE COMPLIMENTS:

1.

2.

3.

4.

5.

## THE "WILDEST DREAMS" QUESTIONS:

1. When did I feel alive today?  (Describe the feeling!)

2. What did I love today? And who/what loved me?

3. When did time fly today?

4. What are my dreams?

## ANSWERS TO MY MORNING QUESTIONS:

**Answer 1:**

What is it about *that?*

How does it make me feel?

**Answer 2:**

What is it about *that?*

How does it make me feel?

**Answer 3:**

What is it about *that?*

How does it make me feel?

**Answer 4:**

What is it about *that?*

How does it make me feel?

**Answer 5:**

What is it about *that?*

How does it make me feel?

## TWO CHALLENGING TASKS FOR TODAY:

1.

2.

# DATE _____

EVENING WRAP-UP:

FIVE COMPLIMENTS:

1.

2.

3.

4.

5.

## THE "WILDEST DREAMS" QUESTIONS:

1. When did I feel alive today?  (Describe the feeling!)



2. What did I love today? And who/what loved me?



3. When did time fly today?



4. What are my dreams?

## ANSWERS TO MY MORNING QUESTIONS:

**Answer 1:**

What is it about *that?*

How does it make me feel?

**Answer 2:**

What is it about *that?*

How does it make me feel?

**Answer 3:**

What is it about *that?*

How does it make me feel?

**Answer 4:**

What is it about *that?*

How does it make me feel?

**Answer 5:**

What is it about *that?*

How does it make me feel?

## TWO CHALLENGING TASKS FOR TODAY:

1.

2.

# DATE _____

EVENING WRAP-UP:

FIVE COMPLIMENTS:

1.

2.

3.

4.

5.

## THE "WILDEST DREAMS" QUESTIONS:

1. When did I feel alive today?  (Describe the feeling!)



2. What did I love today? And who/what loved me?



3. When did time fly today?



4. What are my dreams?

## ANSWERS TO MY MORNING QUESTIONS:

**Answer 1:**

What is it about *that?*

How does it make me feel?

**Answer 2:**

What is it about *that?*

How does it make me feel?

**Answer 3:**

What is it about *that?*

How does it make me feel?

**Answer 4:**

What is it about *that?*

How does it make me feel?

**Answer 5:**

What is it about *that?*

How does it make me feel?

## TWO CHALLENGING TASKS FOR TODAY:

1.

2.

# DATE _____

EVENING WRAP-UP:

FIVE COMPLIMENTS:

1.

2.

3.

4.

5.

## THE "WILDEST DREAMS" QUESTIONS:

1. When did I feel alive today?  (Describe the feeling!)

2. What did I love today? And who/what loved me?

3. When did time fly today?

4. What are my dreams?

## ANSWERS TO MY MORNING QUESTIONS:

**Answer 1:**

What is it about *that?*

How does it make me feel?

**Answer 2:**

What is it about *that?*

How does it make me feel?

**Answer 3:**

What is it about *that?*

How does it make me feel?

**Answer 4:**

What is it about *that?*

How does it make me feel?

**Answer 5:**

What is it about *that?*

How does it make me feel?

## TWO CHALLENGING TASKS FOR TODAY:

1.

2.

# DATE _____

EVENING WRAP-UP:

FIVE COMPLIMENTS:

1.

2.

3.

4.

5.


## THE "WILDEST DREAMS" QUESTIONS:

1. When did I feel alive today?  (Describe the feeling!)



2. What did I love today? And who/what loved me?



3. When did time fly today?



4. What are my dreams?

## ANSWERS TO MY MORNING QUESTIONS:

**Answer 1:**

What is it about *that?*

How does it make me feel?

**Answer 2:**

What is it about *that?*

How does it make me feel?

**Answer 3:**

What is it about *that?*

How does it make me feel?

**Answer 4:**

What is it about *that?*

How does it make me feel?

**Answer 5:**

What is it about *that?*

How does it make me feel?

## TWO CHALLENGING TASKS FOR TODAY:

1.

2.

# DATE _____

EVENING WRAP-UP:

FIVE COMPLIMENTS:

1.

2.

3.

4.

5.


THE "WILDEST DREAMS" QUESTIONS:

1. When did I feel alive today?  (Describe the feeling!)


2. What did I love today? And who/what loved me?


3. When did time fly today?


4. What are my dreams?

## ANSWERS TO MY MORNING QUESTIONS:

**Answer 1:**

What is it about *that?*

How does it make me feel?

**Answer 2:**

What is it about *that?*

How does it make me feel?

**Answer 3:**

What is it about *that?*

How does it make me feel?

**Answer 4:**

What is it about *that?*

How does it make me feel?

**Answer 5:**

What is it about *that?*

How does it make me feel?


## TWO CHALLENGING TASKS FOR TODAY:

1.

2.

# DATE _____

EVENING WRAP-UP:

FIVE COMPLIMENTS:

1.

2.

3.

4.

5.

## THE "WILDEST DREAMS" QUESTIONS:

1. When did I feel alive today?  (Describe the feeling!)

2. What did I love today? And who/what loved me?

3. When did time fly today?

4. What are my dreams?

## ANSWERS TO MY MORNING QUESTIONS:

**Answer 1:**

What is it about *that?*

How does it make me feel?

**Answer 2:**

What is it about *that?*

How does it make me feel?

**Answer 3:**

What is it about *that?*

How does it make me feel?

**Answer 4:**

What is it about *that?*

How does it make me feel?

**Answer 5:**

What is it about *that?*

How does it make me feel?

## TWO CHALLENGING TASKS FOR TODAY:

1.

2.

# DATE _____

EVENING WRAP-UP:

FIVE COMPLIMENTS:

1.

2.

3.

4.

5.

## THE "WILDEST DREAMS" QUESTIONS:

1. When did I feel alive today?  (Describe the feeling!)



2. What did I love today? And who/what loved me?



3. When did time fly today?



4. What are my dreams?

## ANSWERS TO MY MORNING QUESTIONS:

**Answer 1:**

What is it about *that?*

How does it make me feel?

**Answer 2:**

What is it about *that?*

How does it make me feel?

**Answer 3:**

What is it about *that?*

How does it make me feel?

**Answer 4:**

What is it about *that?*

How does it make me feel?

**Answer 5:**

What is it about *that?*

How does it make me feel?

## TWO CHALLENGING TASKS FOR TODAY:

1.

2.

# DATE _____

EVENING WRAP-UP:

FIVE COMPLIMENTS:

1.

2.

3.

4.

5.

## THE "WILDEST DREAMS" QUESTIONS:

1. When did I feel alive today?  (Describe the feeling!)

2. What did I love today? And who/what loved me?

3. When did time fly today?

4. What are my dreams?

## ANSWERS TO MY MORNING QUESTIONS:

**Answer 1:**

What is it about *that?*

How does it make me feel?

**Answer 2:**

What is it about *that?*

How does it make me feel?

**Answer 3:**

What is it about *that?*

How does it make me feel?

**Answer 4:**

What is it about *that?*

How does it make me feel?

**Answer 5:**

What is it about *that?*

How does it make me feel?

## TWO CHALLENGING TASKS FOR TODAY:

1.

2.

# DATE _____

EVENING WRAP-UP:

FIVE COMPLIMENTS:

1.

2.

3.

4.

5.

## THE "WILDEST DREAMS" QUESTIONS:

1. When did I feel alive today?  (Describe the feeling!)


2. What did I love today? And who/what loved me?


3. When did time fly today?


4. What are my dreams?

## ANSWERS TO MY MORNING QUESTIONS:

**Answer 1:**

What is it about *that?*

How does it make me feel?

**Answer 2:**

What is it about *that?*

How does it make me feel?

**Answer 3:**

What is it about *that?*

How does it make me feel?

**Answer 4:**

What is it about *that?*

How does it make me feel?

**Answer 5:**

What is it about *that?*

How does it make me feel?

## TWO CHALLENGING TASKS FOR TODAY:

1.

2.

# DATE _____

EVENING WRAP-UP:

FIVE COMPLIMENTS:

1.

2.

3.

4.

5.

## THE "WILDEST DREAMS" QUESTIONS:

1. When did I feel alive today?  (Describe the feeling!)

2. What did I love today? And who/what loved me?

3. When did time fly today?

4. What are my dreams?

## ANSWERS TO MY MORNING QUESTIONS:

**Answer 1:**

What is it about *that?*

How does it make me feel?

**Answer 2:**

What is it about *that?*

How does it make me feel?

**Answer 3:**

What is it about *that?*

How does it make me feel?

**Answer 4:**

What is it about *that?*

How does it make me feel?

**Answer 5:**

What is it about *that?*

How does it make me feel?

## TWO CHALLENGING TASKS FOR TODAY:

1.

2.

# DATE _____

EVENING WRAP-UP:

FIVE COMPLIMENTS:

1.

2.

3.

4.

5.

## THE "WILDEST DREAMS" QUESTIONS:

1. When did I feel alive today?  (Describe the feeling!)

2. What did I love today? And who/what loved me?

3. When did time fly today?

4. What are my dreams?

## ANSWERS TO MY MORNING QUESTIONS:

**Answer 1:**

What is it about *that?*

How does it make me feel?

**Answer 2:**

What is it about *that?*

How does it make me feel?

**Answer 3:**

What is it about *that?*

How does it make me feel?

**Answer 4:**

What is it about *that?*

How does it make me feel?

**Answer 5:**

What is it about *that?*

How does it make me feel?

## TWO CHALLENGING TASKS FOR TODAY:

1.

2.

# DATE _____

EVENING WRAP-UP:

FIVE COMPLIMENTS:

1.

2.

3.

4.

5.

## THE "WILDEST DREAMS" QUESTIONS:

1. When did I feel alive today? (Describe the feeling!)



2. What did I love today? And who/what loved me?



3. When did time fly today?



4. What are my dreams?

## ANSWERS TO MY MORNING QUESTIONS:

**Answer 1:**

What is it about *that?*

How does it make me feel?

**Answer 2:**

What is it about *that?*

How does it make me feel?

**Answer 3:**

What is it about *that?*

How does it make me feel?

**Answer 4:**

What is it about *that?*

How does it make me feel?

**Answer 5:**

What is it about *that?*

How does it make me feel?

## TWO CHALLENGING TASKS FOR TODAY:

1.

2.

# DATE _____

EVENING WRAP-UP:

FIVE COMPLIMENTS:

1.

2.

3.

4.

5.

## THE "WILDEST DREAMS" QUESTIONS:

1. When did I feel alive today?  (Describe the feeling!)

2. What did I love today? And who/what loved me?

3. When did time fly today?

4. What are my dreams?

## ANSWERS TO MY MORNING QUESTIONS:

**Answer 1:**

What is it about *that?*

How does it make me feel?

**Answer 2:**

What is it about *that?*

How does it make me feel?

**Answer 3:**

What is it about *that?*

How does it make me feel?

**Answer 4:**

What is it about *that?*

How does it make me feel?

**Answer 5:**

What is it about *that?*

How does it make me feel?

## TWO CHALLENGING TASKS FOR TODAY:

1.

2.

# DATE _____

EVENING WRAP-UP:

FIVE COMPLIMENTS:

1.

2.

3.

4.

5.

## THE "WILDEST DREAMS" QUESTIONS:

1. When did I feel alive today?  (Describe the feeling!)

2. What did I love today? And who/what loved me?

3. When did time fly today?

4. What are my dreams?

## ANSWERS TO MY MORNING QUESTIONS:

**Answer 1:**

What is it about *that?*

How does it make me feel?

**Answer 2:**

What is it about *that?*

How does it make me feel?

**Answer 3:**

What is it about *that?*

How does it make me feel?

**Answer 4:**

What is it about *that?*

How does it make me feel?

**Answer 5:**

What is it about *that?*

How does it make me feel?

## TWO CHALLENGING TASKS FOR TODAY:

1.

2.

# DATE _____

EVENING WRAP-UP:

FIVE COMPLIMENTS:

1.

2.

3.

4.

5.

## THE "WILDEST DREAMS" QUESTIONS:

1. When did I feel alive today?  (Describe the feeling!)



2. What did I love today? And who/what loved me?



3. When did time fly today?



4. What are my dreams?

## ANSWERS TO MY MORNING QUESTIONS:

**Answer 1:**

What is it about *that?*

How does it make me feel?

**Answer 2:**

What is it about *that?*

How does it make me feel?

**Answer 3:**

What is it about *that?*

How does it make me feel?

**Answer 4:**

What is it about *that?*

How does it make me feel?

**Answer 5:**

What is it about *that?*

How does it make me feel?

## TWO CHALLENGING TASKS FOR TODAY:

1.

2.

# DATE _____

EVENING WRAP-UP:

FIVE COMPLIMENTS:

1.

2.

3.

4.

5.

## THE "WILDEST DREAMS" QUESTIONS:

1. When did I feel alive today?  (Describe the feeling!)



2. What did I love today? And who/what loved me?



3. When did time fly today?



4. What are my dreams?

## ANSWERS TO MY MORNING QUESTIONS:

**Answer 1:**

What is it about *that?*

How does it make me feel?

**Answer 2:**

What is it about *that?*

How does it make me feel?

**Answer 3:**

What is it about *that?*

How does it make me feel?

**Answer 4:**

What is it about *that?*

How does it make me feel?

**Answer 5:**

What is it about *that?*

How does it make me feel?

## TWO CHALLENGING TASKS FOR TODAY:

1.

2.

# DATE _____

EVENING WRAP-UP:

FIVE COMPLIMENTS:

1.

2.

3.

4.

5.

## THE "WILDEST DREAMS" QUESTIONS:

1. When did I feel alive today?  (Describe the feeling!)

2. What did I love today? And who/what loved me?

3. When did time fly today?

4. What are my dreams?

## ANSWERS TO MY MORNING QUESTIONS:

**Answer 1:**

What is it about *that?*

How does it make me feel?

**Answer 2:**

What is it about *that?*

How does it make me feel?

**Answer 3:**

What is it about *that?*

How does it make me feel?

**Answer 4:**

What is it about *that?*

How does it make me feel?

**Answer 5:**

What is it about *that?*

How does it make me feel?

## TWO CHALLENGING TASKS FOR TODAY:

1.

2.

# DATE _____

EVENING WRAP-UP:

FIVE COMPLIMENTS:

1.

2.

3.

4.

5.

## THE "WILDEST DREAMS" QUESTIONS:

1. When did I feel alive today?  (Describe the feeling!)

2. What did I love today? And who/what loved me?

3. When did time fly today?

4. What are my dreams?

## ANSWERS TO MY MORNING QUESTIONS:

**Answer 1:**

What is it about *that?*

How does it make me feel?

**Answer 2:**

What is it about *that?*

How does it make me feel?

**Answer 3:**

What is it about *that?*

How does it make me feel?

**Answer 4:**

What is it about *that?*

How does it make me feel?

**Answer 5:**

What is it about *that?*

How does it make me feel?

## TWO CHALLENGING TASKS FOR TODAY:

1.

2.

# DATE _____

EVENING WRAP-UP:

FIVE COMPLIMENTS:

1.

2.

3.

4.

5.

## THE "WILDEST DREAMS" QUESTIONS:

1. When did I feel alive today?  (Describe the feeling!)

2. What did I love today? And who/what loved me?

3. When did time fly today?

4. What are my dreams?

## ANSWERS TO MY MORNING QUESTIONS:

**Answer 1:**

What is it about *that?*

How does it make me feel?

**Answer 2:**

What is it about *that?*

How does it make me feel?

**Answer 3:**

What is it about *that?*

How does it make me feel?

**Answer 4:**

What is it about *that?*

How does it make me feel?

**Answer 5:**

What is it about *that?*

How does it make me feel?

## TWO CHALLENGING TASKS FOR TODAY:

1.

2.

# DATE _____

EVENING WRAP-UP:

FIVE COMPLIMENTS:

1.

2.

3.

4.

5.

## THE "WILDEST DREAMS" QUESTIONS:

1. When did I feel alive today?  (Describe the feeling!)

2. What did I love today? And who/what loved me?

3. When did time fly today?

4. What are my dreams?

## ANSWERS TO MY MORNING QUESTIONS:

**Answer 1:**

What is it about *that?*

How does it make me feel?

**Answer 2:**

What is it about *that?*

How does it make me feel?

**Answer 3:**

What is it about *that?*

How does it make me feel?

**Answer 4:**

What is it about *that?*

How does it make me feel?

**Answer 5:**

What is it about *that?*

How does it make me feel?

## TWO CHALLENGING TASKS FOR TODAY:

1.

2.

# DATE _____

EVENING WRAP-UP:

FIVE COMPLIMENTS:

1.

2.

3.

4.

5.

## THE "WILDEST DREAMS" QUESTIONS:

1. When did I feel alive today?  (Describe the feeling!)

2. What did I love today? And who/what loved me?

3. When did time fly today?

4. What are my dreams?

## ANSWERS TO MY MORNING QUESTIONS:

**Answer 1:**

What is it about *that?*

How does it make me feel?

**Answer 2:**

What is it about *that?*

How does it make me feel?

**Answer 3:**

What is it about *that?*

How does it make me feel?

**Answer 4:**

What is it about *that?*

How does it make me feel?

**Answer 5:**

What is it about *that?*

How does it make me feel?

## TWO CHALLENGING TASKS FOR TODAY:

1.

2.

# DATE _____

EVENING WRAP-UP:

FIVE COMPLIMENTS:

1.

2.

3.

4.

5.

## THE "WILDEST DREAMS" QUESTIONS:

1. When did I feel alive today?  (Describe the feeling!)




2. What did I love today? And who/what loved me?




3. When did time fly today?




4. What are my dreams?

## ANSWERS TO MY MORNING QUESTIONS:

**Answer 1:**

What is it about *that?*

How does it make me feel?

**Answer 2:**

What is it about *that?*

How does it make me feel?

**Answer 3:**

What is it about *that?*

How does it make me feel?

**Answer 4:**

What is it about *that?*

How does it make me feel?

**Answer 5:**

What is it about *that?*

How does it make me feel?

## TWO CHALLENGING TASKS FOR TODAY:

1.

2.

# DATE _____

EVENING WRAP-UP:

FIVE COMPLIMENTS:

1.

2.

3.

4.

5.

## THE "WILDEST DREAMS" QUESTIONS:

1. When did I feel alive today?  (Describe the feeling!)

2. What did I love today? And who/what loved me?

3. When did time fly today?

4. What are my dreams?

## ANSWERS TO MY MORNING QUESTIONS:

**Answer 1:**

What is it about *that?*

How does it make me feel?

**Answer 2:**

What is it about *that?*

How does it make me feel?

**Answer 3:**

What is it about *that?*

How does it make me feel?

**Answer 4:**

What is it about *that?*

How does it make me feel?

**Answer 5:**

What is it about *that?*

How does it make me feel?

## TWO CHALLENGING TASKS FOR TODAY:

1.

2.

# DATE _____

EVENING WRAP-UP:

FIVE COMPLIMENTS:

1.

2.

3.

4.

5.

## THE "WILDEST DREAMS" QUESTIONS:

1. When did I feel alive today?  (Describe the feeling!)

2. What did I love today? And who/what loved me?

3. When did time fly today?

4. What are my dreams?

## ANSWERS TO MY MORNING QUESTIONS:

**Answer 1:**

What is it about *that?*

How does it make me feel?

**Answer 2:**

What is it about *that?*

How does it make me feel?

**Answer 3:**

What is it about *that?*

How does it make me feel?

**Answer 4:**

What is it about *that?*

How does it make me feel?

**Answer 5:**

What is it about *that?*

How does it make me feel?

## TWO CHALLENGING TASKS FOR TODAY:

1.

2.

# DATE _____

EVENING WRAP-UP:

FIVE COMPLIMENTS:

1.

2.

3.

4.

5.

## THE "WILDEST DREAMS" QUESTIONS:

1. When did I feel alive today?  (Describe the feeling!)

2. What did I love today? And who/what loved me?

3. When did time fly today?

4. What are my dreams?

## ANSWERS TO MY MORNING QUESTIONS:

**Answer 1:**

What is it about *that?*

How does it make me feel?

**Answer 2:**

What is it about *that?*

How does it make me feel?

**Answer 3:**

What is it about *that?*

How does it make me feel?

**Answer 4:**

What is it about *that?*

How does it make me feel?

**Answer 5:**

What is it about *that?*

How does it make me feel?

## TWO CHALLENGING TASKS FOR TODAY:

1.

2.

# DATE _____

EVENING WRAP-UP:

FIVE COMPLIMENTS:

1.

2.

3.

4.

5.

## THE "WILDEST DREAMS" QUESTIONS:

1. When did I feel alive today?  (Describe the feeling!)

2. What did I love today? And who/what loved me?

3. When did time fly today?

4. What are my dreams?

## ANSWERS TO MY MORNING QUESTIONS:

**Answer 1:**

What is it about *that?*

How does it make me feel?

**Answer 2:**

What is it about *that?*

How does it make me feel?

**Answer 3:**

What is it about *that?*

How does it make me feel?

**Answer 4:**

What is it about *that?*

How does it make me feel?

**Answer 5:**

What is it about *that?*

How does it make me feel?

## TWO CHALLENGING TASKS FOR TODAY:

1.

2.

# DATE _____

EVENING WRAP-UP:

FIVE COMPLIMENTS:

1.

2.

3.

4.

5.

## THE "WILDEST DREAMS" QUESTIONS:

1. When did I feel alive today?  (Describe the feeling!)

2. What did I love today? And who/what loved me?

3. When did time fly today?

4. What are my dreams?

## ANSWERS TO MY MORNING QUESTIONS:

**Answer 1:**

What is it about *that?*

How does it make me feel?

**Answer 2:**

What is it about *that?*

How does it make me feel?

**Answer 3:**

What is it about *that?*

How does it make me feel?

**Answer 4:**

What is it about *that?*

How does it make me feel?

**Answer 5:**

What is it about *that?*

How does it make me feel?

## TWO CHALLENGING TASKS FOR TODAY:

1.

2.

# DATE _____

EVENING WRAP-UP:

FIVE COMPLIMENTS:

1.

2.

3.

4.

5.

## THE "WILDEST DREAMS" QUESTIONS:

1. When did I feel alive today?  (Describe the feeling!)



2. What did I love today? And who/what loved me?



3. When did time fly today?



4. What are my dreams?

## ANSWERS TO MY MORNING QUESTIONS:

**Answer 1:**

What is it about *that?*

How does it make me feel?

**Answer 2:**

What is it about *that?*

How does it make me feel?

**Answer 3:**

What is it about *that?*

How does it make me feel?

**Answer 4:**

What is it about *that?*

How does it make me feel?

**Answer 5:**

What is it about *that?*

How does it make me feel?

## TWO CHALLENGING TASKS FOR TODAY:

1.

2.

# DATE _____

EVENING WRAP-UP:

FIVE COMPLIMENTS:

1.

2.

3.

4.

5.

## THE "WILDEST DREAMS" QUESTIONS:

1. When did I feel alive today?  (Describe the feeling!)

2. What did I love today? And who/what loved me?

3. When did time fly today?

4. What are my dreams?

## ANSWERS TO MY MORNING QUESTIONS:

**Answer 1:**

What is it about *that?*

How does it make me feel?

**Answer 2:**

What is it about *that?*

How does it make me feel?

**Answer 3:**

What is it about *that?*

How does it make me feel?

**Answer 4:**

What is it about *that?*

How does it make me feel?

**Answer 5:**

What is it about *that?*

How does it make me feel?

## TWO CHALLENGING TASKS FOR TODAY:

1.

2.

# DATE _____

EVENING WRAP-UP:

FIVE COMPLIMENTS:

1.

2.

3.

4.

5.

## THE "WILDEST DREAMS" QUESTIONS:

1. When did I feel alive today?  (Describe the feeling!)




2. What did I love today? And who/what loved me?




3. When did time fly today?




4. What are my dreams?

## ANSWERS TO MY MORNING QUESTIONS:

**Answer 1:**

What is it about *that?*

How does it make me feel?

**Answer 2:**

What is it about *that?*

How does it make me feel?

**Answer 3:**

What is it about *that?*

How does it make me feel?

**Answer 4:**

What is it about *that?*

How does it make me feel?

**Answer 5:**

What is it about *that?*

How does it make me feel?

## TWO CHALLENGING TASKS FOR TODAY:

1.

2.

# DATE _____

EVENING WRAP-UP:

FIVE COMPLIMENTS:

1.

2.

3.

4.

5.

## THE "WILDEST DREAMS" QUESTIONS:

1. When did I feel alive today?  (Describe the feeling!)


2. What did I love today? And who/what loved me?


3. When did time fly today?


4. What are my dreams?

## ANSWERS TO MY MORNING QUESTIONS:

**Answer 1:**

What is it about *that?*

How does it make me feel?

**Answer 2:**

What is it about *that?*

How does it make me feel?

**Answer 3:**

What is it about *that?*

How does it make me feel?

**Answer 4:**

What is it about *that?*

How does it make me feel?

**Answer 5:**

What is it about *that?*

How does it make me feel?

## TWO CHALLENGING TASKS FOR TODAY:

1.

2.

# DATE _____

EVENING WRAP-UP:

FIVE COMPLIMENTS:

1.

2.

3.

4.

5.

## THE "WILDEST DREAMS" QUESTIONS:

1. When did I feel alive today?  (Describe the feeling!)



2. What did I love today? And who/what loved me?



3. When did time fly today?



4. What are my dreams?

## ANSWERS TO MY MORNING QUESTIONS:

**Answer 1:**

What is it about *that?*

How does it make me feel?

**Answer 2:**

What is it about *that?*

How does it make me feel?

**Answer 3:**

What is it about *that?*

How does it make me feel?

**Answer 4:**

What is it about *that?*

How does it make me feel?

**Answer 5:**

What is it about *that?*

How does it make me feel?

## TWO CHALLENGING TASKS FOR TODAY:

1.

2.

# DATE _____

EVENING WRAP-UP:

FIVE COMPLIMENTS:

1.

2.

3.

4.

5.

## THE "WILDEST DREAMS" QUESTIONS:

1. When did I feel alive today?  (Describe the feeling!)

2. What did I love today? And who/what loved me?

3. When did time fly today?

4. What are my dreams?

## ANSWERS TO MY MORNING QUESTIONS:

**Answer 1:**

What is it about *that?*

How does it make me feel?

**Answer 2:**

What is it about *that?*

How does it make me feel?

**Answer 3:**

What is it about *that?*

How does it make me feel?

**Answer 4:**

What is it about *that?*

How does it make me feel?

**Answer 5:**

What is it about *that?*

How does it make me feel?

## TWO CHALLENGING TASKS FOR TODAY:

1.

2.

# DATE _____

EVENING WRAP-UP:

FIVE COMPLIMENTS:

1.

2.

3.

4.

5.

## THE "WILDEST DREAMS" QUESTIONS:

1. When did I feel alive today?  (Describe the feeling!)

2. What did I love today? And who/what loved me?

3. When did time fly today?

4. What are my dreams?

## ANSWERS TO MY MORNING QUESTIONS:

**Answer 1:**

What is it about *that?*

How does it make me feel?

**Answer 2:**

What is it about *that?*

How does it make me feel?

**Answer 3:**

What is it about *that?*

How does it make me feel?

**Answer 4:**

What is it about *that?*

How does it make me feel?

**Answer 5:**

What is it about *that?*

How does it make me feel?

## TWO CHALLENGING TASKS FOR TODAY:

1.

2.

# DATE _____

EVENING WRAP-UP:

FIVE COMPLIMENTS:

1.

2.

3.

4.

5.

## THE "WILDEST DREAMS" QUESTIONS:

1. When did I feel alive today? (Describe the feeling!)

2. What did I love today? And who/what loved me?

3. When did time fly today?

4. What are my dreams?

## ANSWERS TO MY MORNING QUESTIONS:

**Answer 1:**

What is it about *that?*

How does it make me feel?

**Answer 2:**

What is it about *that?*

How does it make me feel?

**Answer 3:**

What is it about *that?*

How does it make me feel?

**Answer 4:**

What is it about *that?*

How does it make me feel?

**Answer 5:**

What is it about *that?*

How does it make me feel?

## TWO CHALLENGING TASKS FOR TODAY:

1.

2.

# DATE _____

EVENING WRAP-UP:

FIVE COMPLIMENTS:

1.

2.

3.

4.

5.

## THE "WILDEST DREAMS" QUESTIONS:

1 When did I feel alive today?  (Describe the feeling!)

2. What did I love today? And who/what loved me?

3. When did time fly today?

4. What are my dreams?

## ANSWERS TO MY MORNING QUESTIONS:

**Answer 1:**

What is it about *that?*

How does it make me feel?

**Answer 2:**

What is it about *that?*

How does it make me feel?

**Answer 3:**

What is it about *that?*

How does it make me feel?

**Answer 4:**

What is it about *that?*

How does it make me feel?

**Answer 5:**

What is it about *that?*

How does it make me feel?

## TWO CHALLENGING TASKS FOR TODAY:

1.

2.

# DATE _____

EVENING WRAP-UP:

FIVE COMPLIMENTS:

1.

2.

3.

4.

5.

## THE "WILDEST DREAMS" QUESTIONS:

1. When did I feel alive today?  (Describe the feeling!)

2. What did I love today? And who/what loved me?

3. When did time fly today?

4. What are my dreams?

## ANSWERS TO MY MORNING QUESTIONS:

**Answer 1:**

What is it about *that?*

How does it make me feel?

**Answer 2:**

What is it about *that?*

How does it make me feel?

**Answer 3:**

What is it about *that?*

How does it make me feel?

**Answer 4:**

What is it about *that?*

How does it make me feel?

**Answer 5:**

What is it about *that?*

How does it make me feel?

## TWO CHALLENGING TASKS FOR TODAY:

1.

2.

# DATE _____

EVENING WRAP-UP:

FIVE COMPLIMENTS:

1.

2.

3.

4.

5.

## THE "WILDEST DREAMS" QUESTIONS:

1. When did I feel alive today?  (Describe the feeling!)

2. What did I love today? And who/what loved me?

3. When did time fly today?

4. What are my dreams?

## ANSWERS TO MY MORNING QUESTIONS:

**Answer 1:**

What is it about *that?*

How does it make me feel?

**Answer 2:**

What is it about *that?*

How does it make me feel?

**Answer 3:**

What is it about *that?*

How does it make me feel?

**Answer 4:**

What is it about *that?*

How does it make me feel?

**Answer 5:**

What is it about *that?*

How does it make me feel?

## TWO CHALLENGING TASKS FOR TODAY:

1.

2.

# DATE _____

EVENING WRAP-UP:

FIVE COMPLIMENTS:

1.

2.

3.

4.

5.

## THE "WILDEST DREAMS" QUESTIONS:

1. When did I feel alive today?  (Describe the feeling!)

2. What did I love today? And who/what loved me?

3. When did time fly today?

4. What are my dreams?

## ANSWERS TO MY MORNING QUESTIONS:

**Answer 1:**

What is it about *that?*

How does it make me feel?

**Answer 2:**

What is it about *that?*

How does it make me feel?

**Answer 3:**

What is it about *that?*

How does it make me feel?

**Answer 4:**

What is it about *that?*

How does it make me feel?

**Answer 5:**

What is it about *that?*

How does it make me feel?

## TWO CHALLENGING TASKS FOR TODAY:

1.

2.

# DATE _____

EVENING WRAP-UP:

FIVE COMPLIMENTS:

1.

2.

3.

4.

5.

## THE "WILDEST DREAMS" QUESTIONS:

1. When did I feel alive today?  (Describe the feeling!)




2. What did I love today? And who/what loved me?




3. When did time fly today?




4. What are my dreams?

## ANSWERS TO MY MORNING QUESTIONS:

**Answer 1:**

What is it about *that?*

How does it make me feel?

**Answer 2:**

What is it about *that?*

How does it make me feel?

**Answer 3:**

What is it about *that?*

How does it make me feel?

**Answer 4:**

What is it about *that?*

How does it make me feel?

**Answer 5:**

What is it about *that?*

How does it make me feel?

## TWO CHALLENGING TASKS FOR TODAY:

1.

2.

# DATE _____

EVENING WRAP-UP:

FIVE COMPLIMENTS:

1.

2.

3.

4.

5.

## THE "WILDEST DREAMS" QUESTIONS:

1  When did I feel alive today?  (Describe the feeling!)



2. What did I love today? And who/what loved me?



3. When did time fly today?



4. What are my dreams?

## ANSWERS TO MY MORNING QUESTIONS:

**Answer 1:**

What is it about *that?*

How does it make me feel?

**Answer 2:**

What is it about *that?*

How does it make me feel?

**Answer 3:**

What is it about *that?*

How does it make me feel?

**Answer 4:**

What is it about *that?*

How does it make me feel?

**Answer 5:**

What is it about *that?*

How does it make me feel?

## TWO CHALLENGING TASKS FOR TODAY:

1.

2.

# DATE _____

EVENING WRAP-UP:

FIVE COMPLIMENTS:

1.

2.

3.

4.

5.

## THE "WILDEST DREAMS" QUESTIONS:

1  When did I feel alive today?  (Describe the feeling!)

2. What did I love today? And who/what loved me?

3. When did time fly today?

4. What are my dreams?

## ANSWERS TO MY MORNING QUESTIONS:

**Answer 1:**

What is it about *that?*

How does it make me feel?

**Answer 2:**

What is it about *that?*

How does it make me feel?

**Answer 3:**

What is it about *that?*

How does it make me feel?

**Answer 4:**

What is it about *that?*

How does it make me feel?

**Answer 5:**

What is it about *that?*

How does it make me feel?

## TWO CHALLENGING TASKS FOR TODAY:

1.

2.

# DATE _____

EVENING WRAP-UP:

FIVE COMPLIMENTS:

1.

2.

3.

4.

5.

## THE "WILDEST DREAMS" QUESTIONS:

1. When did I feel alive today?  (Describe the feeling!)

2. What did I love today? And who/what loved me?

3. When did time fly today?

4. What are my dreams?

## ANSWERS TO MY MORNING QUESTIONS:

**Answer 1:**

What is it about *that?*

How does it make me feel?

**Answer 2:**

What is it about *that?*

How does it make me feel?

**Answer 3:**

What is it about *that?*

How does it make me feel?

**Answer 4:**

What is it about *that?*

How does it make me feel?

**Answer 5:**

What is it about *that?*

How does it make me feel?

## TWO CHALLENGING TASKS FOR TODAY:

1.

2.

# DATE _____

EVENING WRAP-UP:

FIVE COMPLIMENTS:

1.

2.

3.

4.

5.

## THE "WILDEST DREAMS" QUESTIONS:

1. When did I feel alive today?  (Describe the feeling!)




2. What did I love today? And who/what loved me?




3. When did time fly today?




4. What are my dreams?

## ANSWERS TO MY MORNING QUESTIONS:

**Answer 1:**

What is it about *that?*

How does it make me feel?

**Answer 2:**

What is it about *that?*

How does it make me feel?

**Answer 3:**

What is it about *that?*

How does it make me feel?

**Answer 4:**

What is it about *that?*

How does it make me feel?

**Answer 5:**

What is it about *that?*

How does it make me feel?

## TWO CHALLENGING TASKS FOR TODAY:

1.

2.

# DATE _____

EVENING WRAP-UP:

FIVE COMPLIMENTS:

1.

2.

3.

4.

5.

## THE "WILDEST DREAMS" QUESTIONS:

1. When did I feel alive today?  (Describe the feeling!)

2. What did I love today? And who/what loved me?

3. When did time fly today?

4. What are my dreams?

## ANSWERS TO MY MORNING QUESTIONS:

**Answer 1:**

What is it about *that?*

How does it make me feel?

**Answer 2:**

What is it about *that?*

How does it make me feel?

**Answer 3:**

What is it about *that?*

How does it make me feel?

**Answer 4:**

What is it about *that?*

How does it make me feel?

**Answer 5:**

What is it about *that?*

How does it make me feel?

## TWO CHALLENGING TASKS FOR TODAY:

1.

2.

# DATE _____

EVENING WRAP-UP:

FIVE COMPLIMENTS:

1.

2.

3.

4.

5.

## THE "WILDEST DREAMS" QUESTIONS:

1. When did I feel alive today?  (Describe the feeling!)

2. What did I love today? And who/what loved me?

3. When did time fly today?

4. What are my dreams?

## ANSWERS TO MY MORNING QUESTIONS:

**Answer 1:**

What is it about *that?*

How does it make me feel?

**Answer 2:**

What is it about *that?*

How does it make me feel?

**Answer 3:**

What is it about *that?*

How does it make me feel?

**Answer 4:**

What is it about *that?*

How does it make me feel?

**Answer 5:**

What is it about *that?*

How does it make me feel?

## TWO CHALLENGING TASKS FOR TODAY:

1.

2.

# DATE _____

EVENING WRAP-UP:

FIVE COMPLIMENTS:

1.

2.

3.

4.

5.

## THE "WILDEST DREAMS" QUESTIONS:

1. When did I feel alive today?  (Describe the feeling!)

2. What did I love today? And who/what loved me?

3. When did time fly today?

4. What are my dreams?

## ANSWERS TO MY MORNING QUESTIONS:

**Answer 1:**

What is it about *that?*

How does it make me feel?

**Answer 2:**

What is it about *that?*

How does it make me feel?

**Answer 3:**

What is it about *that?*

How does it make me feel?

**Answer 4:**

What is it about *that?*

How does it make me feel?

**Answer 5:**

What is it about *that?*

How does it make me feel?

## TWO CHALLENGING TASKS FOR TODAY:

1.

2.

# DATE _____

EVENING WRAP-UP:

FIVE COMPLIMENTS:

1.

2.

3.

4.

5.

## THE "WILDEST DREAMS" QUESTIONS:

1. When did I feel alive today?  (Describe the feeling!)

2. What did I love today? And who/what loved me?

3. When did time fly today?

4. What are my dreams?

## ANSWERS TO MY MORNING QUESTIONS:

**Answer 1:**

What is it about *that?*

How does it make me feel?

**Answer 2:**

What is it about *that?*

How does it make me feel?

**Answer 3:**

What is it about *that?*

How does it make me feel?

**Answer 4:**

What is it about *that?*

How does it make me feel?

**Answer 5:**

What is it about *that?*

How does it make me feel?

## TWO CHALLENGING TASKS FOR TODAY:

1.

2.

# DATE _____

EVENING WRAP-UP:

FIVE COMPLIMENTS::

1.

2.

3.

4.

5.

## THE "WILDEST DREAMS" QUESTIONS:

1. When did I feel alive today? (Describe the feeling!)




2. What did I love today? And who/what loved me?




3. When did time fly today?




4. What are my dreams?

"Formulate and stamp indelibly on your mind a mental picture of yourself as succeeding. Hold it tenaciously. Never permit it to fade. Your mind will seek to develop the picture."

—NORMAN VINCENT PEALE

**CONGRATULATIONS** on successfully completing your journey...*now keep going!*

You've established an AMAZING journal routine that's taken you *far*. The longer you carry on this practice, the more extraordinary your life will become! We encourage you to continue beginning and ending your days with life-changing questions designed to support you in fulfilling the life of your dreams.

If you'd like a shiny new book to keep up your momentum and growth, you can always purchase a copy on Amazon.com. Signed editions are available on our website: www.TheJourneyToAbundance.com

## THE ADVENTURE CONTINUES...

SCAN THE CODE TO FEEL THE
LOVE AND JOIN THE FUN!

EVER-CHANGING. VISIT OFTEN.

WWW.THEJOURNEYTOABUNDANCE.COM
MOTIVATION • INSPIRATION • HEALING • HUMOR

# IN CASE YOU MISSED IT:

# THE ADVENTURE CONTINUES.

## SCAN THE CODE TO FEEL THE LOVE AND JOIN THE FUN!

EVER-CHANGING. VISIT OFTEN.

WWW.THEJOURNEYTOABUNDANCE.COM

MOTIVATION • INSPIRATION • HEALING • HUMOR

Made in the USA
Middletown, DE
09 December 2017